Through the website I had several dozen people contact
 me with various needs from overdue power bills,
this one being that
everything comes from my own pocket
and donations are no longer asked for
and rarely accepted is harder for me but I have
always said if I could do more, I would,
 Id love to help people pay off their homes, buy them new cars, Basically be
the gay Oprah/Ellen...wait...The Gay MALE oprah or Ellen.
    They are truly my inspirations for this, having watched
both of their shows for many years and having
seen them shower people with gifts, love and compassion is what started
me on this path.

After about a year, I was contacted by Dateline NBC's Chris Hansen
who wanted to run a story on me which was about the
wild wild web, strange ads and stories on Craigslist,
 they had run across my ad for helping people online and wanted to
see if I was pulling a scam or was legit.
   They came and interviewed me and did their investigation and the story
never aired.   I found out later that it
 would have only aired had they found out
I was scamming people, since I was
not, there was really no reason to air it.
    I was legit!   I could have told them that though.

A few months later my mom was diagnosed with terminal cancer
 and I was forced to go be with her for several weeks at
a hospice in Kingman Arizona.
 While there I found out that they
 often had patients whose families would visit and
who would need to call long distance
 so they could always use calling cards,
I went to the store and bought Ten $10
cards and bought some books for their
library which was for overnight guests
 who wanted to read and relax. The idea
of delivering flowers to hospital and hospice
patients who didnt have anyone to visit them was born, there are so many
people are sick or dying that
 are alone and who have no one to look after them except strangers.

My Mom died.
    And I began to mourn in the worst way possible,
I got drunk a lot and alienated a lot of people, this is
where I said I am human earlier and
I have many people that cant forgive this time of my life,
 not that I have always
been an angel since quitting the booze
but if there is a message here that I want to convey,
 its love which for me
should include forgiveness.

     I wont get second chances with those I have lost
 but maybe its not too late for you or
for you to find someone in your life who needs it and give it to them?
     Life is short, too short to be without
the people that matter the most to us, even if we are super mad at
someone.

In 2012, I completed that list of things
I wanted to do in my community,
 it is as follows: Donate time and money to
local causes I believe in.
 I found a Paw Pantry which I feel every town should
have in Kingman Arizona while I was
there, this is ran by my friend Kourtney and
 can be found at: https://www.facebook.com/groups/1448393292140448/
    Please
Join her, if you need dog or cat food, ask and you
 shall be helped, if you can help her with donations I am sure they
would be greatly appreciated, she is on my
 list to help when I can and she has helped me with The Wish List even
though
I would never ask for help, I prefer to do this all out of my own pocket!
  Pride? Ego?

I started carrying around envelopes with Cash,
 Gift cards, Grocery cards, Pet cards, Gift Cards and Gas cards so that
when I was out & about and saw someone in need or someone
 who had just shown an incredible act of compassion towards
someone else, I could hand them an envelope and walk away,
 I did everything anonymously back then, I didnt want praise,
I didnt want the person to offer me something
 in return but now when I do this I hand out a business card that
explains
The Wish List in detail so that if the person
wants to come and thank me, they can or if they know someone in need,
they
can send them my way.

Another thing I do is carry around water
 in my backpack, here in Las Vegas,
 it gets very hot in the summer and I am
always seeing a homeless person who
looks as if they are in need or people sitting at a bus
 stop and I know they are
grateful to have the cold drink,
 its just an idea for you, depending on where you live, if its
 cold where you are, how
about buying some hot cocoa at Mcdonalds and offering it to strangers?

I decided to expand The Giving to Boxes.
  I now collect tote boxes and fill them with food, clothes,
 toys, dog food
and supplies, cat food and supplies and baby
food and supplies and when I have something available I announce it on

ï»¿This booklet is purchased and sent out with every Wish List related gift sent from
Amazon but you can purchase a copy of the booklet from Amazon.com for yourself or
your friends, family, church etc to spread the word that I am out there.

The cost of the booklet will be kept very low in case you want to do this.

The Wish List is an out of pocket "charity" though non official,
 that I started in 2009.
  It started out with a call
for help from an elderly woman who had been robbed,
 she called my friend Maria who lived four doors down
 and said that
all of the gifts she had bought her grandchildren,
her tree, basically everything in the garage had been taken,
 as I
listened intently to the call between my friend and this woman,
 I heard Maria say that she was sorry
and she hoped things
would get better, no offer to help the woman,
just an apology and a hope for the future.

I realized in that moment that I had to be the hope that the woman was looking for.
  I placed an ad the next day to
find someone to help me,
someone with a car since I do not have one and a call was answered
by a nice couple who loved
my idea to help this woman out.
 We bought a Christmas tree for her and several toys and delivered them,
 the woman
was so happy that she told her friends about us
and soon I was getting emails from people who needed Christmas trees
and toys for their children and food for the holiday.

I remember taking some toys to a house,
I said to the friend that I felt like this had the potential to draw users and
those that would abuse our kindness and then I saw the house
we were taking the toys to, now they say not to judge a book
by its cover but this house was worn down and needed a
 really good paint job, inside I found a woman in a wheelchair
who had the money to buy a tree and food but had no way
to get to her destination, she tried to pay us and we refused.

Soon we were delivering Christmas trees and toys and food
 all over the Las Vegas Valley.

It was about this time that my mom called me to tell me
that she had found some homeless people living inside the storage
facility that she was the manager of, they had somehow

found themselves an empty unit and had a made a home of it, my
mom believing as I did, after all, she raised me,
decided that she would let them stay and buy them some housewares.

Blankets, pillows and even a heater for cold desert nights.
 I decided to take my love of helping people to the next
level and invited them to my apt for Christmas dinner,
 I love to cook as well so this just felt like the right thing to
do. When word got out that I was holding a
Christmas dinner for the homeless, donations started pouring in,
 someone
donated two pies, blankets for them so when they returned
to the storage unit they would have warmth, several boxes
of food also came in for us to cook and by us, I mean the
homeless men and women wanted to cook with me, they wanted
to contribute!   I was amazed!

I let them take showers and a couple of them spent
the night on my living room floor.   And then Christmas was over...
And I thought...What next?
 And The Wish List was born.
 I was reading a book called The Wish List about finding
out what your deepest dreams are
 and making them happen and
 I besides getting my food out there for the world to try and
my stories published or produced to dvd,
I didnt have that many personal dreams
but I did want to make my corner of the
world a better place, to spread joy and
love and compassion to others, to make
 people feel good, to make people smile
and to encourage them to do the same and
in that moment I realized my mission here on Earth.

I created a website on Facebook to attract people to the movement.
 https://www.facebook.com/Thewishlisted/   And I
began to compile a list of some of the things
 I wanted to do for other people.   This handbook lists them later on!

Slowly but surely people began to take
 notice and the page began getting LIKES.
 I also connected with quite a few
people in need.
One woman needed food so
I emptied my cupboards and gave her what I had.
 I should note here that I am
not writing this Guidebook to get people to oooh and awww over me.
   What I do is because it brings me great pleasure
and is my deepest passion to do for others when I can,
 what people think of me cannot be a concern, I have people that
love me deeply and some that dont feel nearly
quite that way, I am human, I have made some mistakes with friends but
my mission remains the same, make amends, do my best, spread love, help
others!

my site listed earlier and see who wants to come over and pick it up.

Having the experience I had in the hospice with flowers
 for those who were sick, I decided to expand this to local
businesses, now I take boquets of flowers and
homemade or store bought goodies if I have
 been treated well at a pet
store or Vet's office, doctors's office or
 insurance agency, anywhere that I have been where I was treated with
loving kindness, I remember it and make
 sure that the person is later rewarded for it.

I plan to hide treasure boxes when I get moved
 to Oregon which is my home and where I want to be,
 Imagine walking in
a local park or on the beach and coming
across a treasure box and inside is cash
 or a gift card?   I plan to leave
Laundry cards at my local apartment
 complex for anyone who may need a
little extra help and If I can find a local
senior citizen home or apartment
that has a community room, I plan to buy
food and put it in their community fridge.

Another thing that I do is carry ziploc bags
 of mini tooth brushes, toothpaste and deoderant,
 among other things in my
backpack and hand it to the homeless when I see them,
 I also have filled up a box and left it in the offices of weekly
or extended stay apartments here in Vegas,
this way when someone comes into the lobby
 to pay their rent or get a soda
they can take whatever they may need.

In 2013, I decided to add my Facebook friends into The Wish List
 and so I created a Pay It Forward Gift Giveaways
Program on my personal Page..   At random times during any given week,
I may announce a Wish List Gift that anyone in the Group can
win, the idea is to keep whatever You like
 and can use or share it with someone around You or if You cannot use
it or do not want to keep it for whatever
reasons, You can pay it forward to someone else.

The Gifts are totally random as they are decided by a random source
and can range from candles to food boxes to boxes
of candy to kitchen appliances. They can also range between $5 and
$150 but on occasion, They may be worth more.

 The only rule I set in place is that because the gift
 is a secret until it arrives
to your doorstep, you must take a pic or video
 of it when it arrives or if you are inept at
such things, ask me to post

the original link to the gift and put it
 on The Group wall for everyone to see, tell us
what you think of this item and what
you plan to do with it.   I have had
some people complain about these rules and
 I look at it like Christmas-You open
your gift in front of your friends and
 family and share with us your thoughts.
 The winners are also chosen at random
to keep it fair.

Also during the week other surprises can come up,
 here are SOME of them:

Announced Gifts, This is where I post
 a link to a gift I want to send and
 if you want it, You simply say Yes, the first
12 people to say they want it will be up to win it.

Bonus Gifts, I simply announce that I am sending someone again
chosen at random an extra gift.
   And remember these gifts may be things you
cannot use at all such as winning a box
of baby food and I know you dont have a baby!

Recipes, I love to cook and I am always posting
 pictures of my food on my wall, friends have asked me for recipes and
I usually say no, this is a family secret
 but I decided to start sending my recipes out on 3x5 cards at random.
If you want to see any recipe that I have sent to you, I will gladly
post a pic of it as I take pictures and save them of every single
recipe I cook.

Greeting cards, a friend of mine suggested during
a Christmas that she was going to send out Cards
 to people to let
them know how loved they were and I said to her,
 why not do that year round?   Send out cards that
 say, you are loved,
you are special and so you may win
 one of these and there may be just a card
 or something special inside as well, you
just never know with The Wish List.

I also send care packages from Etsy,
 Cracker Barrel, Amazon and Ebay.
 While you do have to give me a mailing address
so you have a chance to win,
 Most every item comes directly from one
 of those companies and your information is always
kept safe and private, I am also not likely
 to show up at your door in the middle of the night,
though if you hear
a rustling in the bushes....

You may also get some cash in your mailbox!
   I am always thinking of new things
I can do for my Members and for the
community at large and ask that you do the same,
 look around you for things you can do, donate school
 supplies, donate
to an animal shelter, make sandwiches
 and take them to the homeless in the park down the street,
 buy the person lunch
behind you in the drive thru.
and again remember, you might be Oprah Winfrey herself and
not NEED $50 in cash but what about someone around you, can
they use it?

Literally anyone with the spirit of compassion and the belief
in paying it forward can join the Wish List and make a difference.

One thing a lot of people do not think about when giving is Household
Items.
   I often will gather several packages
of napkins, toilet paper, paper towels,
cleaning supplies and things along these lines and box them up and send
them
out.

To Join The Wish List: https://www.facebook.com/terry.mitchell.524
But remember you must send Me your mailing address within 24 hours of
joining
or you will be deleted, You cant win if I have nowhere to send the Gifts!
You can also post to my wall when you are added and ask my existing wish
listers
if you can trust me with a mailing address, I have had theirs for 4+
years and
I have never shown up at their door, at least not without an invitation!

My Long term Goal is to get a van or a truck,
 maybe an RV and Hire a driver since I do not drive and travel around
from city to city, much like Oprah's
dreams come true bus and help people in need,
 surprise people with gifts, take
them to dinner, let them have a night in a hotel,
 buy their kids clothes, deliver food boxes and home cooked meals
and whatever else we can fit in that van.

Id love to do a food truck since I love to cook
 and simply feed people who were hungry or run a soup kitchen, I dont
know, I have ideas and dreams but not sure where to take them!

Other ideas?

Take Hot chocolate to the girls on Fremont street.
   I am sure your town has a Fremont street, this is where the working
girls are.

Take calling cards to the homeless
 or homeless teens so they can call home.

Take Hot chocolate to construction
 workers on a cold day or water/soda to them
on a hot day and dont forget the road
crews that are out there.

I also pay attention to people who need medications that
they themselves cannot afford, in fact I am always
listening to people's conversations, looking around me to find
those in need, I pay attention when the woman at the library
drops all of her books and a man rushes over to help her, that
is an act of compassion, that man will get an invitation to The
Wish List.

Scour the ads on Craigslist and find
 people giving away free stuff,
go pick them up and deliver them to other people
in need of those free items!

I also like to do social experiments.
 I will ask for someone to buy me a drink
outside of a Mcdonalds or a Taco Bell
and when they do, give them a gift card
 for the place I am standing outside of. Grocery stores,
Gas stations, Starbucks,
Subway, You name it, this works Great,
sometimes I admit though, I want to tell the people
 that said no what they missed
out on!   Maybe tell them to be less judgemental
and more open to the next person that asks for help

Hey, maybe I can have some business cards made up that say,
 You snooze, You lose.

One last thing on my mind.

For those that have told me they dont need nor want gifts.
  The Wish List isnt about YOU. Its about me helping You
help someone around You. Maybe you dont want that candle, fine.
 Give it to someone else and tell them about The
Wish List, hand them this booklet and keep the movement going.
I know I have said this a lot but this is the #1 excuse I hear
from people for not wanting to Join the Group--I dont need
Gifts, I dont want gifts to be your friend, I dont want for
money...Im rich, Im a celebrity and I have all of the money/gifts
I need...so?   Your point?

____
FAQ (The 26 most asked questions)

1. Where do you get the money to do all of this?

Its 100% out of my own pocket.
 I never ask for donations and I rarely accept them.

2. Rarely but I can send something if I want to help?
Yes...my email address is Irishwaterz@Inbox.com
    You can send me an Amazon card, since most gifts come from Amazon
this will help me out a bit, if you know me pretty well,
I will give you a mailing address where you can send gift
cards of other varieties or homemade items you think may be
useful to others.

3. Do you need volunteers?
Yes!   I do not have a car so I am always looking
 for someone who is local to help me pick up items that I have seen
in the FREE section of Craigslist for example and
drop them off to those in need, I also like to take things around
to local senior homes and hospitals and a car would
 be a great chance for me to be able to do more, thank you!

4. How often can I come to your charity for help?
As often as you need to but because I am a private
 person who is doing this completely or near completely on my own
I wont always be able to help but if I can, I certainly will.

5. What kinds of gifts can I win?
You name it!   I have given away towels, candles,
 candle holders, fudge, juice, bells, baby food,
 its totally random
so anything on Amazon, Etsy or Ebay is possible
 and sometimes I will send items from Cracker Barrel or
some other kind
of specialty shop.

6. How are the gifts/winners chosen?
Well, This is a bit complicated and might take
 a whole other booklet to explain, though that does
 sound like a good idea
now that I think about it...
In my spirituality Dice are used as
a guide to lead a person to new experiences, new directions
in their lives and so I decided to simply
 let the dice choose the gifts and winners
and oddly enough, the dice always
picks the right person and the right gift that matches
up to that person.

7. Im Vegan or Gluten Free or allergic to this item...
Ok, so you pay it forward to someone else who isnt
and give them a copy of this booklet,
 dont forget that part!

8. How do I KNOW for sure you are doing what you
 say you are doing?
Dateline NBC can be contacted but beyond that you

can watch videos of gifts I have sent out and
contact the tagged
winners to see if they really won something,
 You can also check out the comments section
of The Wish List homepage
and talk to some of the people I have helped out.

9. Is their a limit to what you will send?
No.   Its random, your gift can be $1 or $100.
 No way to know.   You can also win much more expensive Gifts.

10. These are a lot of rules just to help people!
   Just common sense rules really--My goal here is to bring
people together, to form a community of like minded individuals
who all care about each other and the concept of paying it
forward. If someone isnt communicating or isnt posting
pictures when they win, that tells me they arent interested
in the community I am offering and so they get the axe!

11. I dont care about Gifts, I just want to be your friend!
If you really wanted to be my friend,
 You would care about me and support
what I believe in, The Wish List, You would
participate in it because its up to you
 to find people to spread this message to,
 people that I do not have access to
in your area.   There should be no excuses,
 you either are in or you are out.

12. Can I ask you for specific things?
No. Gifts are chosen at random remember,
I do bonus gifts though and you never know
 what I will send next but they
are not requested items, also like
any other kind of gift, whether you get
a recipe or a $250 money order, I expect a
picture to be posted on my wall!

13. This sounds like a ploy to get more
 friends/arent you just buying friends?
Well, No, If that were true then I would never delete friends
and when they delete me for some reason, I would offer them
a gift to return, that simply has never been the case, you
dont want to be my friend, let me show you the window...um
I mean the door!

14. What are your spiritual beliefs?
Since I do consider myself a very deeply spiritual guy and
I talk about my beliefs on a regular basis on my wall, I suppose
this is a valid question I should answer. I generally consider
myself to be a Solitary Eclectic Pagan. I revere and honor Ara
or the creative Universal Energy that exists in all things. I
practice prayer, meditation, positive thinking, spirit dancing,
Creative Visualization, Contemplation, affirmations and denials,

Magic and The Sacred Journey which is using meditation books that
have been written for my family and casting dice to know which
direction we should go next in our lives.   However I do sometimes
post about articles, essays and such that catch my eye, this may
be about Jesus, Satanism, Taoism, Zen, Buddhism or many other
paths because I consider all paths valid and to contain some truth
wisdom and knowlege.   I recently began meditating with Mala Beads
due to reading a book about Buddhism, I guess I am saying I am super
open minded!

If you read the teachings from The Center for spiritual Living, My
beliefs
and practices match theirs pretty much to the letter, maybe a few slight
differences, I dont know but I do agree with most everything I have read
from them and its why I support them whenever I can with donations and
Voluntary efforts.

I also would love to attend a local Unitarian Universalist because they
are diverse and open minded, standing on the side of love makes a lot of
sense to me.   Read the 7 Tenents.   But most of all I would say my
religion
is action-Love and compassion in action, I try not to judge, I try not to
condemn, I try to practice forgiveness...

15. I am ________, Would I be welcome in your Group?
Yes!   We have Gay and Straight,
 Black and White, Hispanic and Asian, Transgender
 and No Gender, Muslim and Christian,
Atheist and Satanist and everyone in between,
in fact if someone doesnt understand that we need
to be tolerant of others
and spread love, they find themselves booted out very quickly!

16. I am well known or a celebrity...
Good for you!   You can still Join!
 You can pay your winning item forward maybe
 to a fan or someone that comes into
your restaurant if you have one or you can
 give it to your mom or sister or best friend,
 I would love it for a celebrity
to join The Wish List, no...not so I can
get your autograph or photo, I couldnt care less
 about that, one I want to
get to know YOU, who you are,
what you are about and two, Maybe you
 can hand out the handbooks to some other celebrities
and get the word spreading around about my
project, it will only work long term if I have
support and word of mouth.
You in?

17. It all sounds great but I am leery about
 sharing my personal address with a stranger...

Well...Its kept private 100%, Id never
share it without your permission and I am
never going to show up at your door, You
are also free to ask anyone currently on
 the list if I have ever shown up at their door.
   I simply need an address so
I can tell Amazon or Etsy (etc) where to send your item.
    What is that noise coming from the bushes?

18. What if the rules change, suddenly donations
are required or it ends up costing money or...
You can simply leave. Honestly though, if I
 havent changed the rules, I am not likely ever going to.

19. I forgot to give you an updated address!
Thats bad!
     It would explain though
 why Jennifer Aniston got your gift today!
   No, seriously though, You need to
remember when you move, make sure I have
 a current address on file, I do pay attention
 to friends when they announce
a change but not everyone is so open
 about moving and I cant always keep up,
  sometimes though if someone wins I havent
heard from in a long while, I will check in and make sure!

20. I dont want to send you a donation
 but I do want to send you a personal gift!
I wont deny my friends this if they
are someone I know and they want to
 send one but please remember, I dont personally
need nor want gifts, I am not doing
 this for what you can give back to me,
  I am doing this for what I can do for you
or those around you!   But thanks!
 I keep every gift, if its something spiritual,
 it goes on or near my Altar. smile.

21. How do you know someone isnt using you
 for gifts or just sitting on your list waiting to win?
So what if they are? As long as
 they follow the rules
(Post a pic when the gift arrives, Tell us what they think of
it, tell us what they plan to do with it-keep,
 share or pay forward and hand someone a copy of this handbook) let them
use me away!

22. Can I drop off a food/clothing/toy etc donation to you?
Yes...But because I am not
an official charity but instead a private party,
 I can give you no tax credit or deductions
for it. Just a thank you.

23. Why do some gifts take so long to reach me after
you announce that I won?
I dont always order Amazon Prime "Two" day delivery,
 It can be that your item was ordered from Ebay, Etsy, Cracker
barrel, The of the month club or any number of Import sources.
  Since its a surprise before it arrives, I can never
tell you the why of the delay but Gifts always arrive
and if they do not (and this has happened) I will send you a
new personally picked out Gift.

24. Does the dice choose all of the gifts, always?
Only the random wish list gifts.
 Bonus Gifts are chosen by me but the die
 chooses the winner. Announced Gifts may or
may not be chosen by me but again the winner
 is always chosen by the die to make it fair
so that everyone has a chance
to win.

25. But..I have been on the list for
 months/years and have yet to win!
The die chooses the winner randomly and
 you can watch how it happens in any of
 the videos that are released. Not always
am I able to do a video but when I can,
 I show the process. Unfortunately as the
list grows and more people join, the
odds of you winning decrease but on one side of this,
 I believe the right winner and the right gift are always matched
up, on the other side of it, You should want
people around you to be feel joy and so if
 you dont win but a friend does,
thats good right?

26. You keep calling your personal page a group...Its not a group!
Its a group of people that all believe in paying it forward and making
the world a better place, Its a personal community of like minded
souls but no its not an official "Group".

Bonus Question: Wasnt there a Group once?
Yes, it sucked.   :)   It was impersonal and uncomfortable.
It wasnt ME.

____

Reasons you should avoid The Wish List.

You do not believe in Love, Joy and Compassion.
You do not believe in helping other people.
You cannot be tolerant of alternative lifestyles,
 religions or cultures.
You are a my way or the highway kind of person,
 It just wont work, sorry.
You are just looking to win gifts and have no

intention to pay forward the things you dont like.
You are just looking to win gifts-The winners
are chosen at random, You could be waiting a LONG time!

____

Background

Oh Boy!

Well, I will say that I have been there done that
 and a lot of the reasons I do what I do is because
 I have been through
it, as my Uncle Randy used to say.
  I was in an abusive relationship
 and I could see no way out, I have been low
income and in need of food boxes
 and been turned down because they have a once
a month rule, I have had to travel from
church to church in hopes that I could find one
 that would bend that rule for me, I have gone to soup kitchens for help
and why I support http://www.fcclebanon.org/soup-kitchen.php
    I grew up in Lebanon, Oregon and will always consider
it my home and many of those in The Wish List Group are from
 or live in Lebanon now!

I was also homeless for a couple of years,
 I had to find clothes and food in dumpsters,
 rely on the salvation army for
sandwiches and water, I remember one time
 I was really sick and it was a very hot day,
 I had change, about $2 and I asked
this woman who was heading into the market
 if she would mind buying me some milk and
I tried to hand her my change and
she just stepped over me like I was trash
 and I will never forget that feeling,
 if someone asks me for help and I can
help them, I am going to do that and I
am asking you to think about other people
 and help when you can, My mom used to
say that its not our place to judge people,
 we dont know their stories, we dont know why
they are in the positions that
they are in but we do know that they are a
 human being and that they are asking for
 our help and we can help them so we
should!

I am also disabled.
  I have Fibromyalgia and I am on a
limited income and Yes, after rent and bills
 and groceries are
taken care of, I use whatever
 is left to help others, I have what I need at

    that point so why not?   I am not looking
for praise or recognition, I am simply looking
for new members who are interested in winning
 some nice things for
themselves or to spread to someone else and
 to awaken people a little bit to the idea that
 YOU alone can make a HUGE
difference for someone else!

I write books, short stories and plays now.
  I also write tv series which could be adapted
 to the stage which is one
of my dreams. I would take every penny
  that I made from these things (other than what the theater
would naturally
want for fees and rental costs and such)
 and use it for The Wish List. If I won a million dollars,
 Id buy a small cabin
in the woods near a creek and a set of train
 tracks of course and Id use every last dollar
 to make sure people had
enough food, clothes and happiness to go around.

But...I am not perfect...
I have made some mistakes in my life,
 I have had moments of my own selfishness to contend with
and I have said and done some things
 that have alienated friends and family,
 I only mention this here because you may
join and then hear something about me that
 shines a different light upon me and I fully admit...
Some things they say
may be accurate.

But that only brings us back to
love and compassion because if
 you are showing true love and true compassion, you may
want to also show forgiveness.
 Id love a second chance with the people
 I have wronged or neglected in my life, maybe
someday they will show up ready to truly forgive me, maybe they wont.
   Maybe while you are sitting there listening to
how I wasnt the best friend to them, you can tell them I deserve
 a second chance!

____

So here is the thing.

Amazon wont let me self publish this booklet unless its 24 pages long.

You and I both know that I cannot write 24 pages about the wish
list because what more can I say?

I have said it all.   Show love, compassion,

forgivess, mercy.

Spread Joy and Happiness.

I sound like a Christian eh?

Im not.

So....Besides writing endless one liners,
 What can I put in those last 24 pages?

Poems I have written?

Recipes I plan to share with Ya'll down the line?

Previews of some of my stories?

My personal wish list?

That one is simple!

Meet Ellen, Meet Oprah.
Meet Denise Crosby (Star Trek)
Meet Belinda Carlisle
Live in a nice cabin (have security) Near a creek and a set of train
tracks!
Make a happy life for all abused and abandoned animals
Feed people, help the homeless, Give good advice to help
 people be happier.
Lose and maintain weight loss
Find a spiritual community to be a long lasting part of
Cook fabulous meals and have people come over and eat
Get my writing published or produced
Be truly loved (not by a man, Just by a good friend)
Move somewhere that I can be finally settled.

That is my Wish List...

That is all I desire!

____

Here are some links to Groups on Facebook,
 charities and Pages I want you to support,
some have already been mentioned!

Thesatanictemple.com
I think they are a wonderful voice in the wilderness
for all outsiders whether it be Gays or Muslims, Women or Transgendered
folk, we
all deserve to be treated with honor & respect. Justice is very
important and I
am a firm believer in the separation of church and state and The Satanic
Temple

works for this on a daily basis, Yes, they are a bit overdramatic at times but
you have to admit, they get attention, they are always in the news and they get
results.   Take some time to read the FAQ on their website so you can understand that
they do not kill babies or eat cats.

UUA.org
This is the Unitarian Universalist church, there is always a project going on that
can be donated to, find something that matches your interests or find a local
church and ask them what they are doing presently for their community.

https://csl.thankyou4caring.org/pages/development/general-donation-form-new
   Center for spiritual living
I have a practice in my path called The Sacred Journey, I may have
mentioned this already but if not...The teachings from the
group above are so similar to The SJ, Positive thinking, affirmations
and denials, prayer, meditation, focusing on having the best life
we can have, doing for others, improving yourself so I feel as if
they deserve some donations whenever I can help

http://www.fcclebanon.org/soup-kitchen.php
  The Lebanon Oregon soup Kitchen
While I do not live in Lebanon, someday maybe
 and I have never personally been helped by them, I know that the work
they do in the community is priceless, they can use
 cash donations or you can donate time or other goods such as bringing
them boxes of canned goods (non expired please).

https://www.facebook.com/groups/1448393292140448/
 The Paw Pantry
The woman who runs this group loves to help animals
 and even works in a Vet's office!
    And is a member of The
Wish List and another personal friend.
  You can donate bags of dog and cat food
or money to her directly or join
the group and see what else you might be able to do.

http://www.oprah.com/index.html
 Oprah Winfreys website
From Oprah I learned the joy of living
 my best life, the Joy of helping people
 less fortunate than myself and even
though I myself am low income, I can always
be a beacon of light for someone else,
even if its just a hug or an ear
to listen. Oprah is what
started this drive in me to be a better
 person and then eventually to make the world a better

place, on the shocking chance that you
 are not familiar with her, now is your chance!

http://www.ellentv.com/
 The Ellen Degeneres Show
From Ellen I learned to laugh
 at myself. And to dance.
 And to have fun with life.
And between her and Oprah, I
realized what I can do for
other people with all of her giveaways and surprises,
 I wish I could do as much but I am
doing my best!   Take a look at her spirit!

https://www.fmcpaware.org/aboutfibromyalgia.html
        Fibromyalgia awareness site!
Please spread awareness about this illness.
 I have this and I suffer from being tired
 all of the time to being cranky
and moody, having anxety to having acid
reflux to Irritable bowel syndrome and
 aches and pains in my body, I am dealing
with gum pain and tailbone pain today.
  Its not a fun illness to have and its not
 made up or all in my head, its very
VERY real and VERY Painful.

http://thehungercoalition.org/wordpress/about-us/our-story/
  Blaine county (Ketchum/Hailey Idaho) Food bank
This is from what I understand a traveling food bank,
 exactly what I want to do long term and in my quest to find
a place to live, I somehow came across Hailey Idaho,
 I think its connected to the center for spiritual living
which is here or more accurately between Hailey and Ketchum.
   I started researching for food banks and places that
The Wish List could get involved with and this came up
and I LOVE everything about them so please, donate to them
Tell them about The Wish List, if you are in Blaine county,
 take them a copy of this handbook...I may just end up
in that area and be able to do more long term, I dont know
 where I am moving yet.

http://www.southlincolnresources.org/waldport-food-share.htm
 Waldport Oregon food, appliance and clothing share
This town also has a BIKE share for people who need to get
around and dont already own a bike or a car! How amazing is
that? You can get furniture from them, clothing, food
and appliances, this is an amazing place and they even have
medical equipment if you are in need, I want you to
 donate to them for sure!

https://www.cancer.org/involved/donate.html
  American cancer society.
Having lost my mom, grandmother and Aunt Helen to

cancer, this is always on my mind so please donate,
 participate in
cancer runs and walks, wear a pink ribbon to show
 support for cancer victims and their families.
 Visit a hospice
or cancer ward and sit and hold the hands of patients
 that are alone.

https://www.facebook.com/pages/Joan-Diana-Hospice/243819579120775
  The hospice in Kingman Arizona where my mom died
Ever so often I will show up and give them flowers or candy,
 last year I took them a ceramic angel to put by the
front desk. They always need books for their library
 and calling cards so people who are there can call their
friends and families long distance.
    Please do what you can. Volunteer
your time if that is all you can do.

https://www.gofundme.com/ Go fund me.
I love this site but I am always looking
for the honest stories, I have seen too
 many people asking for things that they
really didnt need or people claiming to
 have cancer and it turns out to be a scam,
 I would look for the woman who
honestly says she wants money for a trip to Europe or a
 man who says he wants to take his wife on a nice honeymoon,
these may seem like selfish requests but they are honest ones.
    You can always research the people who are making
requests as well by Googling their names or checking out
their Facebook accounts, ask around!

Note*

There are several groups and organizations I donate to that are not
listed
I either cannot think of them at the moment or something new will crop
up and that will become something I choose to focus on but you will
always know what is going on if you are a member of the group...I
hide Nothing.

https://www.facebook.com/Thewishlisted/
 The Wish List page.
If you need help, this is the place to go!
  If I can do something for you, I will.
 As you may notice on the page
The donation button has been disabled.
This is because if you really want to donate
 you can contact me below (The
next link) and we can discuss it but as I have
 said before, you should be warned, I dont need donations,
 drivers yes..
Volunteers absolutely but donations..Not
so much...But if you are persausive enough...

https://www.facebook.com/groups/290348044737867/
The Transitioning Vegan.   I am the least judgemental
person you will ever meet and I am a homecook and I love
food but I was in a 90 day Vegan challenge and met the
wonderful woman who runs this group, she is also a member
of our Wish List group and believes in paying it forward to
others, If this is something you believe in, that animals
are not here for food or you just want to learn some wonderful
new recipes or cooking ideas, join in!   I myself am Veganish
I learned to make my own cheese, Nice cream, smoothies but
I still cook and eat meat on occasion and Eggs/Honey.

https://www.facebook.com/terry.mitchell.524
    The group of course!
____

How are gifts/winners chosen exactly?

You can find out by watching a Video
on my page, it explains in it detail
 but basically I have 6 lists on my cell phone
with 36 gifts listed in each section,
 I roll, lets say a 2 so list #2...Gift #52
    And thats what I send.   11-66 is
36 Gifts Just in case you are confused,
as Piper would say from Charmed, dont bother
 trying to understand me or the dice
You'll just get a headache!

When I get to the Amazon or Etsy
 Page where your type of Gift is,
 I roll to see what page your gift is on...Lets say
the die says Page 1, and what row is it in?
  Row 1?   ok...There are 3 gifts per row if
 you know much about Amazon..
which of the 3 Gifts? 5...so thats the 3rd Gift over.

Who wins?

I go to the Friends list
  There are two rows of members...
I roll 1-3 LEFT row... 4-6 RIGHT row.   2 Left row.
  OK
Top or Bottom of the left row?   1-3 TOP
  4-6 BOTTOM 1 ok TOP...and then I will
 roll on each name starting at the
TOP till I roll a 1 and that is the winner,
 at least this is how the wish list gift winners are decided.

Bonus Gifts are chosen by ME but the winner is
 still chosen in the same way.

Announced Gifts are chosen by ME

and if you want it, You put YES in the comments,
 the first 6 people are able to compete
for the Gift, The die chooses 1-6 and that
 is the person that wins.   If we dont have
at least 6 people that want the
Gift, No one wins but thats not usually the case!

Have a headache yet Piper?

SMILE

The Die is a VERY Important part of
 my life based on how I was raised and its
 likely very random but I dont think that
it matters at all. Lets say there is
a lesson to learn about patience and
 I am sent to practice YOGA and The die is
random and I go to the Yoga studio
 and I meet some fantastic new friends
 who want to help with The Wish List, Great!

Now, lets say the die isnt random and its all ordained by Ara
 (or God). I still get to the Yoga studio, I still meet
some new friends and they still want to help with the wish list.
   Did it matter if the die was random? No, not one
bit!

Some friends believe that they are the right winners
 for the right Gift and thats fine, I sometimes
 think that too, In
fact I think I mentioned this earlier but
 some believe its all just luck and randomness
 and thats ok too, I dont get
hung up on details too much.

I also use the die in several other areas of my life.

Writing
Cooking
Eating Out
Travel (Dice road trips)
The Sacred Journey (my spiritual practice)
Minor finances
    (You will see this touched on a little below)

Kind of like Tao.   That which can be described is not Tao.

Some Quotes from The Sacred Journey that are important to me:

"I love You, I Bless You, I appreciate You"
        ~The Road to Love~

"I give thanks for my spiritual family"
        ~The Road to Ara~

"I Give up Unproductive thinking, I am in the right place at the right
time"
          ~The Road to Wisdom~

"Because I have a caring attitude, I have a Vital life and care about
others"
          ~The Road to Compassion~

"Joy is in my heart"
          ~The Road to Life~

____

In closing I think for me the
 most important thing to hold
 on to is that No matter what
 Path we are on we should strive
to be a light to others.
   I want to leave a living memory,
 I want people to think of me and say, wow, he really changed
my life in a good way, I am
 uplifted and thats not always
 a mission I have accomplished but I am a work im progress,
much like my Vegan Transition,
 I always say "Progress Not Perfection"
 and that is true on so many levels for me!

____

One last question I was just asked by someone and I think its
a pretty good one!

#27 What are some kinds of posts You will make on a daily basis?
and do I need to communicate/Participate to be in the Group?

Memes...

Food posts...

Recipes, while you can win recipes-Both a regular and Vegan
version will be sent to you if you win.

Spiritual posts, I dont often talk about religion but If I see
an article of interest I will post it.

Q&A--I want to get to know YOU and you me...and I do this by
asking questions on occasion. You do not have to answer
every question that I ask but if you are sitting there without
a word for weeks at a time, you wont last long, I may see that
as being there just to win a gift.

You can also post:

Anything that is positive and uplifting.

Videos of people doing compassionate deeds for other people
such as social experiments where people give money to the
homeless or Ellen (one of my 2 idols) surprises someone with
a new house or car...

Causes you believe in, perhaps I will see something that piques
my interest and I can add this to the list of places or people
that I am willing to help?

Basically anything that makes us feel good and does not push a
personal agenda such as your religion or your lifestyle, not to
say you cannot post something inspirational such as an example:

Knowing You are divive, show divine love to others. That is very
nice, doesnt appear preachy and allows for everyone to have their
own personal understanding of what is divine :)

Id also love to hear YOUR stories, YOUR experiences, things you
have done or are doing to make the world a better place, Your
Groups that are PRO Pay it Forward.

Dont just wait for me to announce something!

Have at it!

____

Testimonies (Much appreciated for adding this one in guys
...Though I dont want nor need praise, I do need to make this
a 24 page booklet, haha)

Terry helped me and my family with a crib
 and some high chairs, we just moved here and
 I found out I was pregnant and
we didnt have anything and the wish list helped!   G

yes I won The Wish list, and it is a favorite
 of mine, and no he never asked for anything in return. N

I have known Terry for years and
 he is the type that would give
 up everything he has to help someone out, Ive never
won the wish list but I have
 won much more by having him as a friend,
though no he is not perfect, he has made some
serious mistakes   N

I have won the wish list several
 times and I am not even on facebook   S

I will be honest,
 I have never won the wish list

  and I have only known Terry for a year or so but he is super
generous, he offered to buy me
  a fan when it got very hot in
my house and last week he offered to buy me some dishes
who does that?   P

One night I was being beaten by my
  at the time boyfriend, I called Terry
  at 5am and he walked over to my apt which was
at the time about 4 miles from his house
  and he stayed with me, sat with me all
  morning, thats who he is!   A

Terry is a great guy, a little weird
, he is quirky but who wants plain jane, not me!   M

I have been sent random gifts,
  not even wish list winnings,
just one day opened my mailbox and there was a gift and I
found out its from Terry, he thinks of others like that.   D

Terry is far from perfect,
  he did something a few months
  ago that really caused some damage to our friendship, in his
words "I went too far"
   that he did but I am
working on forgiving him,
he has a good heart but like anyone else he
is human and makes mistakes.
   And admitting what you did wrong
and trying to make amends is BIG with me! Anonymous

I just met Terry in a vegan group,
he really cares about his health and
the lives of animals, he isnt vegan yet but
I believe he will get there someday
  and that shows he has a good heart that
  includes animals and people but one thing
I have noticed and please forgive me,
  he hasnt the best self esteem,
  I dont honestly think he believes himself to be
good person and that is why he doesnt
  like praise, just my opinion though!   C

Terry wont take help from anyone
  so you have to be sneaky and ask
  one of his other friends for his information, other
than that, he is great!   N

Warning, Terry will delete
  you if you do not participate
  in the wish list, his page, his rules, just saying   R

———————————

Thanks for reading!